Look Again

A Collection of Poems from the Heart and Soul

Patricia Alexander

Look Again

This Book is Dedicated to

Everyone Who has Ever Known What It Means to Love...
Truly and Unconditionally!

The Love that is not rational, intelligent or intellectual!
But Beautiful, Illogical and Fairy Tale!

And to those that have loved me the same way!!

Table of Contents

A Moment

Time goes by too quickly
as I lie here with you
Your fingers trace paths of hope
on my skin so gently
As I write lines of poetry in my heart
my mind cannot keep up
Words fail me as your heart beats
in sync with mine
Your eyes speak truths only I can see
in these moments that never escape me
When silence becomes the most beautiful sound
I have ever heard
I could spend lifetimes
painting my love upon your skin
As I touch your face one last time
for the first time once again
So sacred you are to me
as I thank the God who has brought us together
Smiling as I kiss you like I never will again
missing you before I'm even gone
You have taken me at my best
and forgiven me at my worst
Yet still you love me
like no one ever has
I stare at you in wonderment
amazed that I could love someone so much
I am in love with all that you are to me...
And all that I am when I am with you!!!

As I Sit Here Alone

I am following the trails of purple skies…
to the wings of orange flames that illuminate the passion of love ignited in my
soul.
For you and only you.

And though I am alone in the deepest sea…
of the bluest ocean of beauty and countless dreams.
I am never without you.

For I am shameless in the moment that I fall for you…
over the light of the soft shining moon in the darkness that hides my devotion.
Night after night.

And our secret remains…
through the poetry of invisible words.
Written on pages that only our eyes can see.

And as I sit here alone…
I know I am not.

For you know my love is no secret from within your heart.

Awaken

My mind has erased the memories of days lost into the darkness of discontent.
Like fallen leaves in winter, they lie helpless and brittle…
Awaiting the elements to shatter them into tiny pieces,
until the wind carries them off never to be seen again.
As branches reach for the sun, I too reach for you!
New blooms find their way to unfold carefully in the dawn of a new day…
My tears fall softly like the summer rain,
covering uncertainty and despair that no longer threatens this life
This day becomes the beginning of everything beautiful in this world.
Everything beautiful that you are and have always been to me…
Though I have neglected to see you with my eyes…
I see you now
And flowers bloom within the seed you have planted in my heart
Petals reaching towards the heaven I have come to believe in with you
And my mind is free …
Free to feel love and desire that I have clouded with reality…
a reality not for the weak
but for those strong enough to be bonded for life
As my spirit awakens … and I rise above the clouds,
I finally realize…
I have never needed my eyes to see …
Nor my mind to believe…
What my heart has felt all along
What my soul will never forget again!
What reality can never take away
From you and me!

Confusion

I walk with heavy footsteps in the shadow of a forbidden world that I am finally convinced I will never understand
I am forced within truths that I quietly shelter from my dreams
The one place where I can close my eyes and become the one who is special in the eyes of a make-believe life

And I have created a different world
where I am convinced that perfection is an attainable feat through countless acts of kindness and sincerity
Only to find that one dim mistake draws our steps further back than the progress made

And maybe I am an unworthy spirit that does not follow the guidelines that were set
And I rewrite the rules to fit the difficult of situations and complexity of reality
No one understands the pain the heart feels when forced into gray areas of life
Where there are no definite roads to follow

And I am never allowed to feel nor speak of the truth
As I am constantly misunderstood
And the idea that good outweighs the bad is only proven false in my eyes
For I have always done far more good that goes unnoticed when all hope fails

And one would likely have given up by now
No sane person could possibly find any goodness in what we endure
yet I travel the same path even with tears in my eyes
again, full of hope that I might one day make no mistakes
And you would only find an Angel of beautiful intentions and meaningful words that is here for you no matter the cost

Confusion con't

But I drift further away
Alone resorting to the believe that it is the only real place I belong
I have forced my way into your heart hoping some day you would truly see the truth in me
And though there are times that I feel you do only to be torn between different worlds that not even I, in my true intentions can make good for you

As I slip thru your fingertips engulfed in the darkest shadows of the deepest abyss, I hope to be found one day illuminated in light that surrounds the intentions of my soul
Promising and reborn in those eyes that looked lovingly into my heart
And forgiven for those uncontrollable emotions that only prove my love comes from the depth of a connection most will never know

And though I cannot make good on every bad moment that tears us apart
I can continue with a weakened heart to do the very best it will allow
Because when I say I Love you...it is the one thing that still stands in the wake of all this confusion

Despair

Out of weakness and despair we find truth sometimes hidden from the reality of our actions

And what seems to be reality of the world we've grown to know is often a perception of what we would like for it to be

You have become the only thing I have ever believed in... ever hoped for... ever dreamt of... ever loved so carefree without reservation

It's been said that we should be careful what we set our hearts on for it will surely be ours

And I have set mine on you!

Maybe too much so that I create this animosity between you and I

And I am to blame for making you my entire world

Where every moment I am wrapped in tender thoughts of who we are together and the person I am with you!

Unimaginable my life is to be without you

Frightened by the concept that one day you will no longer be mine

That I will run you away from me never to be thought of again

As I must have done for thousands of years

But to have found the truth I have found in you leads me deeper into an understanding that no one could ever know

How desperate have I become to fear something so beautiful

That my eyes fall silent in the heartache I create

And to apologize is never enough for I cannot undo what has been done.

I find it hard to breathe as tears fall like raindrops that may never end

My world clouded by darkness and helplessness that no one even knows

How do I go on?

Cradling my head in my hands

How do I face the reality where no one even knows the truth?

How can I live without you? My friend, My love, My life!

Determination

When the dust settles on a year not lost
We find our story remains
Yet a new chapter begins.
Following untraceable steps back to the beginning
of a time, unforgiving to reality,
We carry out a dream we are unable to let go of.
Powerful in our quest not to lose that
which has been placed in our hearts...
What we have come to believe is so strong...
A challenge predetermined by forces unknown
in a world so determined to fall short
in the belief that love could be so magical yet so real.
Outrunning storms that devastate the landscape
so beautifully maintained
by two souls who find strength
to move mountains and divide the earth
just to be close.
When a touch beneath waterfalls
is all that is required to breathe.
And a kiss is forgiving of even the darkest nights
quietly calming a trembling heart.
We live effortlessly in the sound
of each other's voice...
softly comforting the tribulations
of what we attempt to disregard as real.
Falling deeper into oceans of dreams
that sustain our love beyond all that is wonderful.
Determined to make our love defy the rules of reality
And allow us to share that of which few will ever know!

Don't Think

Moments pass by more quickly than I would like
For when the lines diminish and reflections fade into the darkness,
I find an emptiness I've never before known.
Our moans become distant echoes of a fire burning from within...
A place where dreams are only sheltered by the reality, we've come to hide
My breath becomes quick and shivers of your touch upon my skin force my eyes
closed
as my head falls back into the seat.
How I fail miserably at denying the ache in my heart I feel when I am away!
And night becomes my enemy...
torturing my soul to believe in something much more than the eyes can see.
But oh, how I see you, my darling Love!!
Not just in dreams anymore...
but before me in the reality of the world I've come to know
...................with you

For as Many Eternities

I searched for so long
An unending journey thru forests of unknown dreams and false realities
Finding comfort in my solitude was the only thing I really knew
until I saw you standing under the stars.
A light shone bright upon you
but still I spent my days wondering if eons of separation would continue
If I would always love you from a distant star
as far from the sun as we traveled away from one another

And days turned to years,
but you continued to fill my dreams
A hope left lingering
Taunting my understanding of everything I thought I knew
So, I finally reached for you one day
And you happily embraced my soul
Giving meaning to lifetimes of loneliness
I found comfort in your voice
And completeness in your touch
As I had never known

Oceans of dreams becoming a reality before me
when you kissed my soft lips
I am weak in the presence of your love
Falling gently through the winds of sincerity
You opened your heart to sweep me in
Where I swear, I will remain for as many eternities as we create.

Forever

I run to you in the dark of night
Flying through clouds of spiritual reflection
In the eyes of every dream I've ever dreamt
Following footsteps on a path that leads
Straight to your heart.

I travel through forests of visible roadblocks
Meant to deter the faintest of hearts
Yet I find no obstacles in my destination
For my life, my world, my soul
remain forever in the love I have found in you

I will never stop following my heart
To the happiness of who we are
my sacrifice no greater than the love we share
And though our love comes with a price
I gladly pay with a promise to you
To never stop ...
As I forever fall deeper in love with you!

Found

I fly above wings of angels...
In search of silver linings,
That shine beyond dreams.
Take my hand and follow me home
Where we have abandoned all sorrow
And love never dies.
It is here where you found me...
Baptized in the springs of the earth...
Destined to be made new again,
In your eyes.
My soul no longer for sale
For you have paid the price
To save me.
I bow before you.
I offer myself unconditionally
For the sacrifices you have made.
My love unending
And my desire unforgiving
I thirst for nothing so much as you.
for I am in love with a treasure beyond these worlds!
Never again will I fail.
Never again will I settle.
So Please take my hand and lead me home!
For it is there...
Where you found me!!

I Am

I am held together at the seams by the tiniest gestures...
The ones that leave me smiling long after you've gone.
I am the unspoken words you hear when not in sight...
A ghost in a crowd of nonbelievers in the true meaning of love.

The energy I feel when I am surrounded by you is the energy that sustains me when you are far from sight.

I am far more to you than the physical appearance of my skin...
I am the depth your soul feels when you find me alone in your thoughts.
I am the aura of the love that surrounds you in all you do...
The Angel that lifts your spirits and protects you at all costs.

My soul has awakened to the happiness I have found in the quietness of my mind
Where all my thoughts lead back to you.
I am free of fear and uncertainty as I am understanding of all I was once not.

You open my eyes and accept who I am...
I am everything you see that is beautiful.
Yet without you...
I am nothing more than a spec of sand along an ocean of endless dreams.

I am That Girl

I am that girl you always dreamed of
The one who worships you with no condition
I am that girl that loves you through every great moment
And the one who loves you more through every bad one
I am that girl that wishes the very best for you
Even when it is not the best for me
I am that girl that thinks the world of you
Even when the world is not so kind
I am that girl that could make the stars shine for you
Even on the darkest of nights
I am that girl that never for a moment stops thinking of you
Even when my mind is overwhelmed
I am that girl that misses you as soon as you walk away
Even when I know I will see you again soon
I am that girl that can't imagine a life without you
Or stop dreaming of a time that I might be yours
In time I hope you see....
I am that girl that you will always need.

I am Yours

For a moment I see your smile
across crowds of unsuspecting souls
None the wiser to see the sparkle in my eyes
As I smile back.

Quickly looking away as to not get lost
In the one place where I find my true self
A safe sanctuary of peace and serenity
Where sadness does not exist, and I am free to love you and worship you the
only way I know.

And I do not hear the voices surrounding me
You are all I hear...
As I make my way through crowds of meaningless conversation ...
You are all I see

And the long walk towards that smile I crave
Becomes a runway of dreams
As I see us one day.... hand in hand...
Arms wrapped around hopes that have gotten us this far...softly kissing away
fear...
No longer hidden from the reality we have created.

And in that moment of pure happiness
I am free...
I am loved...
I am yours!!!

I Believed in You

I believed in you from the beginning of time...
That my dreams would find shelter in the shadow of faith you have helped me to find
I followed a path most resisted to settle comfortably in the fear most felt
But I am no longer amongst the hopeless and discontent
My heart overflows with a love immeasurable by our time
I am convinced of the immortality of our one true soul
For it is you that finds me beautiful in ways unexplained
And it is I who finds you king of the kingdom once forgotten
Ruled only by truth from within
As I succumb to every emotion ever imagined
No explanations are ever needed
I stand in awe before the man I have waited lifetimes to find
Completely engulfed in a love found only in fairytales
I embrace you for the eternity that we embark upon
And for the moments we may never forget
For within the depths of my soul, I am yours forever.

I Exist Only for You

Sunrise opens windows to a world yet explored
As we find ourselves mirrored in the reflection of a new day
A day within which I live lifetimes in your eyes.
I know your touch without feeling...
your voice without hearing...
your face without seeing ...
for I exist only for you.

In this world left unfamiliar,
I live amongst your dreams....
you have dreamt me into reality.
As my wings unfold, I find serenity in the smallest of places...
with you I am never lost...never alone!

I am the love you have searched tirelessly to find
Sheltered only by situations beyond control
do you hide me away in your heart...
Until we are set free to feel.

As you slowly place your hands around my soul
You hold the power to destroy all that I know....
all that I feel...
all that I have come to be.
And I am not afraid...

For I exist only for you, my love!

I Remember

Do you remember the moment that your heart fell quietly into mine?
When the light of your soul illuminated the darkness of my own...
I remember.
For it is every moment of every day that my heart falls for you...
Deeper in love with every look into your eyes...
Every touch of your hand in mine.
Like the flame of a candle shining brighter in the night
You light the path that keeps me always with you
Dimming the subtle cliffs to either side that threaten to swallow me whole...
Keeping my eyes safely within your faith...
Redirecting my steps to what you know to be true...Your love.
I am stronger than ever because I carry your strength in my belief
And you carry me effortlessly day after day.
Even when my trials are great
And I am burdensome and unreachable
You always reach me and pull me home
Home with you is where I will always belong.
Even when distance separates us and time apart is devastatingly long...
I know where I belong...With you.
As the sun sets quietly over the horizon
And the stars become all the guide I need to find you...
I am mystified still at the story we've come to write...
The story that has no ending...
Only sequels to an abounding love that Ties us to each other forever.
When shadows flicker under the closing of my eyes
and you are all the dream I see
And all the man I need...
I remember...
I remember the moment that I fell in love with you because I do it every day!

I Think About You

Do you know what I think about when I am thinking of you?
I think about how your smile lights up my night and fills my soul
with happiness!
I think about how I hear your laugh and I am reminded of just how beautiful
you are to me
I think about how time falls away too quickly when I am with you and I miss
you as soon as I leave
I think about how sincere and kind you are to me even when I don't deserve it
About how much you care about me and everything I do
I think about how I can count on you when the world is falling apart
I think about how safe I feel when I am with you
I think about how complete my life is with you in it
I think about how blessed I am to have found my soul mate
I think about how long your kiss stays on my lips long after we part
I think about how beautiful I feel when I am lying in your arms and there is
only us
I think about how very much I love you and how every time I look at you, I fall
deeper in love with you
All these things I think about you
Every moment of every day!

I Wonder do You Know

I wonder do you know
That every time I see you smile
I am breathless
Momentarily paralyzed
helpless in my emotions
That find their way to your heart.

And I wonder do you know
How my heart stops beating
Every time I look into your eyes
Blinding my reality that has brought us this far
Unforgiving of anyone or anything
For only you do I see.

And I wonder do you know
How my skin comes alive
Every time your fingers
glide softly across it
Sparking new desires for you
I've never felt.

And I wonder do you know
How my mind finds peace
Every time I hear your voice
When no one else can hear
how softly you speak
Only to me.

I Wonder do You Know con't

I wonder do you know
How beautiful you have made me
by loving me the way you do
And allowing me to love you back
Like no one ever has
Or ever will again.

I wonder baby
Do you know how much I love you?
And only you!
Do you know how nothing has ever mattered to me ...?
Until you!!

I Write

In this life that claims uncertainty of everything we are to become, you and I...
I write so that you may see the faith in my heart and the hope in my eyes
When your words question our destiny,
I write so that you may know we can never go back,
but we will continue to move forward
And that the end will surely justify the journey
I write to remember moments that sustain all we have become
Over the time that has so gloriously lifted my life
To a happiness I can only feel when I am with you
I write that you may feel the blessing you have since become to me
That you may feel my sadness when we are apart
Knowing that it is you I am missing
I write that you may look in a mirror and see that it is me that you see smiling
back at you
That your soul and mine together make who we are
I write so that you may hear the words I share
When it is only you that can hear me
when I am alone in my thoughts of only you
I write that my words will somehow express a deeper understanding of
everything we are
Everything we continue to fight so hard to keep
I write my love so that you may never forget
Just who you are to me...
the love I have come to cherish more than anything
I write because it is then written
without doubt...without question...without condition....
that I will never stop loving you for all eternity!

If Only You Knew

If only you knew
How perfect you have become to me
When I lay my head upon you as the night falls
And I become silent
as we lie in a quiet peace
stopping the time that quickly gets away
Could I stay here forever...
If only you knew
How quiet my mind becomes
When the sky hides the darkness of the past
And all I see is the light of your soul
Even through the bridges that have been burned
And the tears that have flooded the nights alone
Would you still come to me?
If only you knew
The love I have endured
to be one with you even for a moment
To feel your heart beat softly
And whisper words meant only for you
Would you love me forever?
If only you knew
That I cannot stop loving you!!

Imperfect

I live an unrealistic life baby
Sheltered in my dreams and misconceptions
tormented by expectations that no one could possibly meet
though you have more than proven your love to me.

I've hidden behind walls carefully built
by strengths I foolishly convinced myself I had
Relentlessly carrying burdens of stone
under the conviction of others.
Cursed by imperfections I blindly ignored
as no one had the courage to tell me I had.

You have been my savior
though I have continually disappointed you with my thoughts
Selfishly drowning you in my emotional ocean of despair
Unfairly accusing he who has held the key to my heart all along.

Desperate is my soul to find meaning
in the chaos of living
Troubled by what I always believed to be real
Determined to not let reality stand in my way
I naively fight to keep you by my side
Though I know that you deserve more than me.

I make promises I can never seem to keep
Believing that one day I might possibly get it right
And you would smile knowing how hard that I try
But I never do.

Imperfect con't

I have convinced myself that your life has more meaning with me
And at times I really feel like the Angel you deserve
Because all I ever wanted was to be the gift you could not return
Your soul mate you could see in the reflection of you.

But I will never be the measure of a woman you so eagerly sought
I will never be the picture your heart wants to see
I will only be the flawed individual
Imperfect is all I can ever be

And when the tides pull back and the sun no longer shines
I hope the light that you see
Is the Angel you so graciously loved
The Angel you once called me.

Lifted

I'm silent as your wings carry me gently
beyond dimensions of time and space...
To heights that lift my soul above heaven.
Certain of everything yet uncertain of anything.
Overwhelmed by tears I cannot control.
when I can no longer breathe.
And you always find the words
to wash away pain I cannot bear.
And the weight of my soul
Is lifted by the love in your heart.
And in one moment I see only you
Your eyes lit like sun dancing upon the water
And I feel your smile as I become aware
Of just why we are here
and I am tranquil in the peace I find...
sheltered in awe to be loved so completely.

Look Again

A dying star is still a star when streaking across the atmosphere
Look again as it burns brighter towards the end of its existence
lighting up the night sky
Granting hope upon a wish we carelessly took for granted
Continually fighting to dismiss all that has torn us apart
Looking to renew that which has held us in our soulful belief that together we
shine so bright
And the rising sun is still a flame setting awareness in a new day
As the fire burns its way to our unforgiven brokenhearted souls
thirsting for waters in streams left dry and cracked
As the heat tears apart the foundation we had come to stand upon
Lifeless and helpless until the rains fall
Though the clouds find their way to dismiss the drought of our sunken hearts
Heavily sedated in their fate to restore all that we have come to know of beauty
and love
But look again
As the flowers bloom and the birds begin to sing
And the thundering echoes of our pounding hearts refuse to cease
Look again as you feel my love undeniably stronger than ever...
Though weak am I in the presence of yours
For we are elements of earth, heaven and hell
Limitless in our power to sanctify a soul driven love
Poorly prepared to accept a destiny that would test the light of our being
Yet greatly rewarded by the divinity of what our destiny has become
What our love can endure
But if we fail to see our souls in the light of each other's eyes....it is not that
they are not there...

Just look again!

Lost

I wake to a hollow soul
energies drained from painful thoughts
Of questionable intent
Lost in a Paradise of Unfamiliar dreams
Swimming effortlessly in my head
Tiring sighs of torment filled breaths
lost to a life with no meaning
I find no comfort in the flames left burning
through the ashes of discontent
Bleeding veins depleted of that which sustains
the life I've come to know
Colors lost to hope forgotten
And faith diminished in the reflection
Of the love I desperately seek
Yet still my heart beats in unison
With the quiet echoes of the peace
I close my eyes to find
And I see you...

My Heart is Heavy

My heart is heavy...

Weighted by my love for you...Not lost....nor forgotten...Only enduring!

As the distance between us grows

I will not say goodbye! For it is you that I think about...

Unanswered questions quietly put to rest by the sound of your voice in my head.

How I long for the day that you will fully understand your destiny...

Completely trusting my love for you.

You are my balance... All my unsettled soul needs.

If only I could be your flame once more

Your everlasting desire...Your world.

I stare blankly at the scenery flying by

Wondering how you are...

Are you thinking of me too ...

Do you feel me cradle you in my arms?

Holding tight to the faith I have never lost.

Though tested again and again...I will not crack

I am an eternal testament of pure belief in who we are ...

you and I

And I will carry you with me no matter how far I need go

To prove over and over again that some things must be felt to be believed

So feel me now my love as I whisper what you know to be true

I love You...

Desperately...

And eternally...

Because some loves were not meant to change!

No Longer Immortal

Sometimes I am lost in this world that has come to judge those of us they do not understand...
But you have always found me
Carefully they misplace the idea that there are those of us who seek more...
In you I have found more.
And why does everything have to be black and white?
Sometimes there are no clear lines that divide dreams from reality
And why does there have to be?
You are my dream made real.
It's those grey areas in this life that separate us from others
That connect us in ways only felt by true loves
And sometimes the truth abounds leaving uncharted grounds that we stand upon
Only to find it is where we've always stood...
together.
Still no one has all the answers to those questions that warrant our existence
Nor would they believe in them if they knew
They are disturbed by who we really are ...
Those of us who delight in the deviation from life as it is known...
Finding our hearts beat in unison with the soul of each other
When someone means more to us than ourselves
It is a testament of pure faith and adoration in the spirit of unconditional love
And though they try to pull us back further than we've moved forward
They forget to account for the strength of the soul
The souls of those of us who know love
Pure and unconditionally!

Redemption

You might think I'm hopeless
Concealed in vines of misery
Squeezing the life out of everything beautiful you once saw in me
And once lifted by wings that carried me towards you now broken and torn
struggling for freedom to fly again
To redeem who I truly am to you.

And I know Redemption comes at a price that I sometimes lose sight of the true
importance of the light that shines beyond all darkness
though I am sometimes blinded by the brightness of your soul
And the love you truly show.

But your soul still lifts me beyond all that hinders our love and drowns out the
truth that deep in our hearts we both know
I only want you to see the hope still left in me
And feel my love redeemed
For you my one true measure of all that this life has to offer
Are the salvation of all that my soul has yet to give...
To only you!

The Air

I find comfort in the air that surrounds us when we are alone.

Swept under shadows that linger above us.

I am taken back by the story your eyes tell when there is nothing but silence...

And your kiss finds its way to my lips softly anticipating your desire for only me.

I feel powerless beneath you.

As if you were a God whose rightful choice was to choose me.

How humbled I've become believing I am your choice!

I wonder do you fully grasp the magnitude of the love I have for you

As I stand secretly before you in plain sight of a dream come true...

Holding on to the one thing I never lose...hope!

That this foundation will not crack beneath us...

Swallowing up the love that pushes us forward in the light of complexity.

I stand firm in my passion to not let go

Though we struggle for forgiveness of that which attempts to break us...

Only to find bonds become stronger and like a rubber band that does not break

We spring back to that which ties our souls and strengthens our hearts.

Because the air that surrounds us is pure

Untainted or polluted by reality

Breathable by the ones whose footing is solid

Untouchable by those who do not know this love!

The Drive

Moments pass by more quickly than I would like
For when the lines diminish and reflections fade into the darkness,
I find an emptiness I've never before known.
Our moans become distant echoes of a fire burning from within...
A place where dreams are only sheltered by the reality we've come to hide
My breath becomes quick and shivers of your touch upon my skin force my eyes
closed
as my head falls back into the seat.
How I fail miserably at denying the ache in my heart I feel when I am away!
And night becomes my enemy ...
torturing my soul to believe in something much more than the eyes can see.
But oh how I see you, my darling Love!!
Not just in dreams anymore...
but before me in the reality of the world I've come to know
...................with you!

The Journey

I know we are on an unfamiliar road
Traveling with blind eyes
To a destination undetermined
and though we may not always know
where the path leads
The journey fills our hearts
with hope and a love unquestionably
For I need not see the end
to believe in the truth from the beginning
And struggle as we may
on this journey we embarked upon
I just can't help believing
In the dream that we are...
The dream we create
When every moment is filled
With thoughts and hope
of a love only hidden temporarily
in this life that is slowly becoming ours...

The More I am With You, The More I want to Stay

Falling from sight as night draws close...
I find solitude in the dim light over the horizon.
As the fire breathes its last sigh...
embers explode into a spectacular display of color into the night sky.
Alone without you....
yet here with you have I always been.
Where hearts cannot be divided,
and souls combine to create a true meaning to life.
I want for nothing more when I feel your touch...
as my skin becomes alive once again for you and only you.
How beautifully you fill every hollow space of emptiness I've ever felt.
Where I no longer need closed eyes to see my dreams.
And if only I could paint with my heart,
every stroke of my brush would represent an eternity of my love for you.
And the strongest of men would fall helpless
in the wake of a strength unbeknownst to most...
an undying and unending satisfaction of purity that comes only from within.
Eternities have eluded us to bring us here...
In this time where we shelter reality but embrace the timeless truth.

For the more I am with you, the more I want to stay.

The Now

I am unafraid in the presence of you

Unstoppable in this life I have come to understand with you

In these moments there is no questionable doubt where my destiny lies

Though there is no end to this journey

I will stay upon it so long as you will travel it with me

I am yours in the realm of spiritual connections that blanket our lives and pull us forward far more steps than has taken us back.

I do not shadow the now with the darkness of the past nor follow the footsteps into the future...

For you are my now and you are all the need and desire I will ever feel

Walking within your footsteps I will live in this present moment always...

Full of love and understanding for you my one true belief.

That you, my kindred spirit and soul mate are the most significant part of my life, my very purpose for living.

Though we are unexplainable in the eyes of reality, I need not explain it to you.

And shall we walk the muddy waters and torrential rains...

You will only find we still stand upon the highest mountain grounded by what cannot be denied...

We are bound by a love that holds us to the moments that are now...

And I shall live here with you for eternity.

The Sun and the Moon

I Love when the sun can be seen with the moon
And the rain shares the night with the stars...

I Love how the leaves dance with the wind
And the sky kisses the earth from afar.

I Love how your words light the depths of my soul
And quiet the tears in my heart...

I Love when your smile crosses distance between us
And nothing can divide or pull us apart.

With no doubt I continue to live for those times
When everything falls into place...

When in moments your weakness reminds me of truth
At times hidden but never erased.

So, I will say as I do that, I shine within you
Even through tears in the night...

And I'll dance through the storms that blow us apart
Til again we are surrounded by light.

Together

Sometimes this road is difficult
And we turn down a dead-end street.
But somehow,
we see the signs that guide us back safely to where we know we belong
So, we cut our own path
back to where we find the sun still shines for us
Our love is strong and never ending
Even in the wake of frustration and despair
We find comfort in the bond that binds our love and carries us thru.
We are united by our souls that no longer search for our hearts that are no
longer missing.
For together we are everything
existing for a purpose that alone we could never fulfill.

The Wall

I am lost behind a wall.... frightened...
Though I have followed my heart through your flames of despair
unintentionally lit by my own accord
I have forced you to build this wall of stone
out of anger and disappointment
Led by my impeccable nature to be the ground you could stand...
the path you could freely choose...
the destiny you were sure I was...
the love of your life
That you could be certain that your soul could feel mine...
irreversibly...unconditionally
Soulmates in the sense of belief of what is
But I continually upset the flow of the beautiful love we had created
Driving you deeper into an unawareness of who I truly was
And even now when you feel distanced and disconnected from me
I can't help but feel more in love with you
As I struggle to find a way to tear down that wall
And the world can laugh at me if it must
For I don't really accept defeat when it comes to you
Yet I'm horrified by my disposition
to feel insecure and no longer beautiful in the only eyes I've ever lived in...
yours
And if I could only have one more night
Would you look into my eyes and find the truth?
Or am I forever hidden......
Silenced by the words you no longer find
Threatened by the silence I can no longer take

Lost behind the wall I will always be trying to tear down?

This Girl

You know you love this difficult girl who dares to be different ...
seeing you in a brighter light....
loving you from afar....
longing for the moments with you....
laying out her heart for you to see....
pouring out her soul into yours.

She is passionate about her love for you
and the life she has come to know with you
which has been better than any life she's ever known.
She cherishes what you have together but
she sometimes does not know how to handle
so much emotion.

When consumed with so much love for one person
she falls short in understanding and tolerance
and she makes herself crazy.
And when that person can't be with her all the time
her heart spills over and her words become
distressed and desperate.

If you listen closely though you will hear what she is really saying
and you will be humbled to have this girl
who loves you that much
She has learned to express herself to you
sometimes the only way she knows how
and that sometimes comes out poorly
when she speaks.

This Girl con't

She doesn't mean to make you feel bad though,
    only to make you so happy
        that you have this girl in your life that wants for nothing but
you.
        And she knows how you feel about her
            but she is scared like any normal girl would be
                that you might change your mind
            about her when you are away from her.

She misses you terribly when you aren't around
    and just wants to see your eyes look into hers
        to remind her how beautiful she is to you.
            She loves you unconditionally without reservation
                and spends all her time dreaming up ways
                    to make you happy.

She miserably fails at life sometimes
    because she so desperately wants to live the dream
        that you have become to her.
            So, forgive her when she falls,
                she always gets back up
                    and she moves forward
                        never giving up on the one
                    thing she believes in...
You and her!
    You are her soulmate and reason for living!
        She's just this girl after all!

Those of Us

Sometimes I am lost in this world that has come to judge those of us they do not understand...

But you have always found me

Carefully they misplace the idea that there are those of us who seek more...

In you I have found more.

And why does everything have to be black and white?

Sometimes there are no clear lines that divide dreams from reality

And why does there have to be?

You are my dream made real.

It's those grey areas in this life that separate us from others

That connect us in ways only felt by true loves

And sometimes the truth abounds leaving uncharted grounds that we stand upon

Only to find it is where we've always stood...

together.

Still no one has all the answers to those questions that warrant our existence

Nor would they believe in them if they knew

They are disturbed by who we really are ...

Those of us who delight in the deviation from life as it is known...

Finding our hearts beat in unison with the soul of each other

When someone means more to us than ourselves

It is a testament of pure faith and adoration in the spirit of unconditional love

And though they try to pull us back further than we've moved forward

They forget to account for the strength of the soul

The souls of those of us who know love. Pure and unconditionally!

Unforgettable Nights

My body sinks into the softness of my bed
As my spirit follows you home
I feel your head tilt back and your eyes close gently
As I imagine my head on your chest
Reveling in the hours spent with you by my side
Laughing and smiling freely....
Loving you with no conditions....
Holding back nothing.
My body trembling at the thought of your kisses
Left lingering on my lips
And your scent fills my senses
As I close my eyes....
I am complete and unaware of the energies drained by the love we had just made
More in love with who you are to me
More sure of who I am to you
I dream as if continuing this night into the dawn of a beautiful new day...
Knowing your voice is the last I heard...
And the first I will hear again.

Unsettled Night

My eyes burn like fire
From hours of sleepless dreams
I find you alone
sheltered in unforgiving words
Your mind restless....
Your heart longing
For better moments
That are sure to come!

My touch is gentle
As I sweep my fingers across your face
But your smile comes slowly
With reservation
And your eyes are sad reminders
that we are not immortal
but here I can smile for you
Beneath this tree
And you know where we are
It is where we need to be

Time stops if just for a moment
That I may tell you our story
Once again
Heartache and sadness very much
A part of happiness and love
For to bring us to where we have been
We must walk footsteps on earth
We do not understand
And heavy as pain is to bear

Unsettled Night con't

My love for you is weightless
lifted beyond worlds yet explored...
worlds anxious for me to explore
With you!

So, sleep with me my love
My arms hold you close
My heart holds you closer
And my soul bears your soul
For the pieces that we are
Fit the puzzle we have yet to finish
and every opportunity
Whether happy or sad...
Places one more perfect fit
To a picture worth believing in!!!

When the Sun Rises and Sets

When the sun rises and sets between you and I
There is no distance…
No time wasted…
No words unforgiving.
I am honored to be the love you so graciously adore
As you never fail to bring the highest level of beauty into my life
You are the only sun I need to survive my love
My path lit by the guidance you create
You are the only truth I am certain I feel
When I am lost in confusion and overshadowing thoughts
I can smile in the warmth of your heart
Even when I am broken and torn
I am comforted by the sound of your voice
No matter the words spoken
I need no reminding of the love I feel in my heart for you
It is as evident as the stars in the night sky
You are every part of me as I am of you
And I know this to be true…
When the sun rises and sets between you and I!

Why do You Fight it?

The truth follows you wherever you go
Why do you fight it?
I am the softest weakness in your heart
I cannot be hardened by this life with you as my solid foundation
The rock that rolls silently over the highest peak and lowest valley
You, my greatest ocean of longing
For moments I am granted the opportunity to share my soul with you
What is it I do wrong when I have only glorious words that flow from within myself to your heart?
Do you hear me...
When the night is silent, and I cry for this love I have come to embrace?
The tenderness and sweet song of your words that take pain out if every sharp-edged wound
I am every good intention there has ever been for you
I am your light and your salvation from within
Silently patient ...yet outspoken in my heart for only you
Why do you fight it?

Within the Reaches of Heaven

In a moment I am swept within the reaches of heaven...
As the truth unfolding before me becomes all that is precious in your eyes.
And I finally see what you see in me...
That is everything I see in you!
And ties do not bind us nor force us together...
For we are securely bound by forces stronger than we could have ever imagined.
Displaced as we are,
meant for higher destinations, as we have been and always will be called upon
by others.
Yet we found within our hearts the sanctity of a pure love ...
Spiritually fused by the flames that ignite this love
A love that tradition cannot defend
Nor rightly understand beyond the scope of humanity.
We are soulful of our mindset to receive this blessing that nothing in this life
can take away.
For within my heart you shall hear the beating of your own...
And within your soul, I live!
And every beautiful moment shared by you and I,
Is one moment closer within the reaches of heaven.

Without You

I'm just a lonely girl without you
Lost atop this mountain
No longer guided by passion
No inspiration to fire my soul
My words lost on the peaks that diminish my existence
Though my love has not failed you
It fills the canyons below
Flowing endlessly to your heart
Wherever you are,
the river leads only to you
Carrying hopes and dreams long not forgotten
Swift reminders of how much I love you
Oh, how I miss you so
Your smile lifts me and guides me home
And I feel you as the wind blowing through my hair
I stay carefully within the grips of my dreams where I will soon wake to your
voice once more
My world has never ceased to exist until I have lived it without you.

Yearning

Aimlessly wandering through the perception of life
We continually grasp for some unforeseen spirit.

Wanting, needing, wishing for that which completes us.
Always searching for the fulfillment, the love
Never before felt...
Only to find emptiness and sacrifice.

We long for closure in this world...
A sort of completeness.

We strive for the love that may never come
Yet we know is out there.

Maybe in a world we do not recognize.

Could it be that we missed it?
Could we have been so blind?

Or maybe now is not the time...
or maybe...
just maybe...
We are blind.

You Lift me

You lift me up
Where my feet no longer touch the ground
As the sun goes down
On a day I wish would never end
I sit silently…Mesmerized
I believe in our life
I believe in our love
I believe in you
Unable to give you up
I am all yours
Dreamily I search your face
Fascinated by who you are
my soul Burns for you
Ignited by sparks left flying
Between desire and love
Touched from the inside out
I carry you with me
Everywhere I go
Never am I alone
your words speak softly
When I am lost
That you may find me once again
Do you know how I silently pray?
Every time we're together?
Thankful for the moment
That can never be taken away
I love you like I could never have imagined
Like I never will again
In you...I have everything I ever need!!

Your Voice

I have fallen helpless in the sound of your voice...
surrounded by the gentle words left lingering in my Heart.
You speak to me in ways no one else can hear...
touching every part of my being.
Bringing to life the me I have longed to be...
encased by a love only created by you.
I drift effortlessly into your arms...
where you may hide me away for eternity.
Where no one is aware of just how beautiful
you have made me!
My eyes soft starlit reflections of what I see in you.
How I wish you could only see the truth.
I do not tread lightly on what we have been given.
In this life full of difficulties and uncertainty...
I am certain of you!
For your voice speaks to me in ways only my soul understands....
And I will listen forever!!

Acknowledgments

I would like to acknowledge everyone in my life that have inspired me to write the words that have been so carefully placed in the poems in this book. There have been so many people that have touched my life in a way that can only be expressed through poetry. Thank you for allowing me to feel passionate about the things that make me who I am. You all know who you are and what you mean to me in my life.

I wish to acknowledge and thank my kids, who have always been there to put a smile or a laugh in my heart. You have always been the most significant part of my life and I could not imagine my life without you. Thank you for being the greatest gift I was ever given in this life. You each have a beautifully unique heart and soul that makes you who you are to me. I love you all so very much.

Made in the USA
San Bernardino, CA
29 August 2019